THE REASON I WILL BEAT THIS PANDEMIC?

(Because almost all of my Ancestors lived to be 100 years old, except those who died earlier.)

Claude Earl Hooker

TABLE OF CONTENTS

PREFACE

During this pandemic I have come to realize the most important things in life are for me to wake up each morning and know someone cares whether I am alive or dead, whether I am happy or sad, or weather I need to be reminded my continued presence on this earth really matters.

Even though I have come to understand these are the most important things in my life, I have also firmly grasped the realization that during this life-redefining-realignment of society, whether or not I have this recognition from others can't determine or effect, whether I live through this death generating crona virus.

Looking back over my slightly more than seven decades of surviving in what has been a somewhat predictable, though uncertain world, the current unpredictableness of day-to-day life has significantly reduced the probability I can pick up a phone, call someone who will reassure me I am loved and needed, or that I will receive a call, text or email indicating someone I have shown concern for is making sure I am OK.

What I have been convinced of since mid-March of this year is that most people I have provided financial, emotional and personal support to are only concerned weather I am in place to provide more of the same. Calls, emails and texts have come in at a record rate, but clearly not to see if I needed help, but to make sure I can be in place to provide assistance.

Repeatedly, I have been told by callers how the crona virus has negatively affected their jobs, their bank accounts, and their ability to travel and enjoy life. With each call, text or email, I have dared to indicate that my source of income had been affected, that my doctor had indicated I needed an immediate operation and that I personally have all of the conditions placing me squarely in the highest category for not surviving the virus. Not one person did more than say, " . . . haven't heard from you in a long time, just wanted to make sure you are OK. " One caller did leave a message saying, " . . . I am just checking in, wanted to make sure you were OK, be careful, you know there are not many of us left." I didn't find this call comforting at all.

Old friends, current associates,

relatives, objects of my affection who long ago decided their time would be better spent with someone else (anyone except me) have checked in. Testing the waters with a text, one got right to the point, " . . . do you remember me . . . we worked together in 1984, call me I need some help? Another emailed, " . . . call me today after 7 p.m. It doesn't matter how late you get in from work, I will wake up. I need to talk to you." Most notable was the email, " . . . this is very important to me. I can't understand why we can't meet, with the pandemic and you not working, you have plenty of time."

As President Trump said about catching the crona virus, " . . . it is a blessing from God that I experienced it myself, it has been an education, now I understand what this thing is . . ." The pandemic has allowed me to open my eyes and understand who I can definitely depend on to come to me for help when they are in crisis, it has also high-lighted who I can't go to for support, if I am in need myself. Blessing or curse? I am not sure yet, but I am reviewing my friends list and I am checking it twice.

This worldwide death-generating public health crisis has caused me to do two things; (1) reflect on my life and how I have responded or not responded to my friends, and (2) make a list of those who are demonstrating some concern for me and my wellbeing.

I have decided to turn this pandemic into the most productive period of my life. I have reviewed my strengths and I am confident in my ability to confront whatever comes, grow stronger and wiser, and develop new skills and resources that will enable me to grow and prosper in the New World Order.

My ancestors have prepared me for just such a time as this. Going back to my childhood, I have met again with my ancestors in Spirit who dedicated their lives to prepare me for a world that they knew would be ever-changing, discriminatory and hard.

This book will introduce you to the builders of my personal foundation and the people who are now watching over me from the Spirit World and guiding me through this Covid-19 crisis.

I characterize these people as my Family.

Some of my Family members are Family by virtue of blood, and some are Family because of service to me in their specific desire to contribute to my well-being and my ability to survive. These people have taught me there are no disabilities as a result of birth, and that overcoming and achieving is a matter of when and how, but definitely not if.

After well over seven decades of identifying the people who constitute my Family, I find their numbers are very, very few. Their relationships to me are diverse and without any unifying cause or characteristic with the exception of caring whether Claude lived or died.

Some of my Family members I have helped, others I have not. A few have reason to believe I have made positive contributions to their lives, others have assisted me for reasons far outside of my ability to comprehend. However, within the limits of my understanding, I know I have been truly blessed to have had these people in my life.

I started writing this testament to memorialize my Family over fifty years ago. In the late hours of the nights and in the very early hours of the mornings from their places in the ethers, the members of my Family have awakened me. These voices of the long departed have told me they wanted to be included in this book, the temple that will be a monument to their lives.

Great aunts who have guided me as a very small child, departed uncles, cousins, non-related individuals from the community, all great teachers who saw what was lacking in me and wanted to contribute to my life's journey and put me on the path towards honesty and the development of a discerning spirit returned to me again and again in 2020.

My spirit Family has come to me when those on earth with me have turned away. In speaking from the ethers they said, " . . . tell people the things about me Claude that were important in shaping your development, tell them who we were and tell them about the struggles we had to endure to pass through this earthly plane, especially our struggles in assisting you.

The souls of my Family have come to me during this pandemic and they have taken me back through the paths we walked in the deep South when racial discrimination was considered what was suppose to be and what would always be. They have assured me they went through and survived the last worldwide pandemic, and the secrets they have taught me will enable me, not only to survive this pandemic, but also to grow and prosper.

Although my Family is in the Spirit World now, this year, they have re-walked with me through the fields of corn and tobacco, and I have again felt the hot rays of the blistering sun on my face, re-experienced the hot summer days of chopping weeds from corn, hand suckering tobacco and planting potato fields. Reliving these experiences was a long spirit-strengthening journey. It was just what I needed to remind myself of who I am, and why there is nothing I can't survive.

During these super-natural visits from my Family, there have been times their voices and their razor-sharp visual images have made me laugh and smile, but just as often, I have cried and wept uncontrollably. Looking back at the history of discrimination experienced by my Spirit-Guides saddens me, but it also gives me strength during this period when I must seek solutions to new and never before experienced negative situations.

The Spirits of my ancestors have come to me when I wanted them to be present for support, and they have returned when I needed help and didn't realize that I did. They say to me " . . .

Claude remember where you have come from so you will know where you are now and what you have to do to survive." When the pain of remembering was so great I could no longer emotionally stand under the weight, their voices intentionally added more volume. They would say, " . . . Claude remember what I taught you in 1949 as you stood on the front seat of my pickup truck as we road through the dusty fields." The Spirits told me I have been prepared by them for the coming of this world-wide struggle and they have positioned me well to adapt, go forward and come out on the other side stronger, wealthier and healthier.

Many, many, so many times in the last 50 or so years, I have assembled these pages about my Family and have attempted to package them for publication. Now, with the world closed, my Family is forcing me to finish.

At this stage in my life I will either finalize this series of reflections or pass on with the stories untold. If I go into spirit without finishing, these stories will be thrown out with my effects identified as having no value, just the random recollections of the departed. So, before I join those who have given me

the knowledge and strength to take-on
this crona virus and win, I, here and
now, finalize my Family history.

In the following pages you will
find the messages from my Family given
to me through their Spirits. Through re-
ceiving these messages, I have learned
that the Family members I obeyed without question are at peace with me and
with their roles in shaping my life.

My Family taught me that I could
not be the center of everyone's life. That
different Family members had centers in
their own universes that excluded
Claude.

My Family also has taught me to
forgive myself for things I have done
wrong and to forgive others for negative
actions taken against me. In communi-
cating with my Family in the Spirit
World, I have come to better know myself. I have learned who I am, who I
want to be, and what makes me able to
defeat this pandemic, no matter what the
odds.

With the world closed, I have the
once in a 100 year opportunity to stop
and write about my Family, most of
whom lived to be 100 years old, EX-
CEPT THOSE WHO DIED EARLIER.

As you read the following stories, you will hear about my barber Jackson, now deceased some 40 years, who still comes to me at night and says, " . . .Claude, please tell my story so I will not be forgotten." You will laugh or cry, as you read the description of the Guiding-Spirits who have enabled me to survive the downs and the way-downs of life.

Now that my mother and father, their mothers and fathers, my great grand parents and their friends and associates are gone and are no longer available to me, I realize that not being able to either consult, delegate or review important decisions with them is a great loss, but because these people have been in my life, there is no barrier that I can't successfully negotiate.

I have been prepared to triumph over this pandemic by the BEST PEOPLE the world has ever known, MY FAMILY.

CHAPTER ONE

MY GREAT AUNT EDNA

My great aunt Edna was my maternal grandmother's youngest brother's wife. She was a tall woman of substantial dimensions. I remember always looking up at her, not only because of her statue, but because of the kindnesses she showed me. I looked up to her and admired her as a child and I still do so today many years after her death.

I must have been in my late thirties or early forties when my great aunt Edna died. Now thirty-five or forty years later, I can't remember whether I was taller than she was, or whether her mere presence made her a towering figure for me.

I never made any blood distinctions making one of my relatives closer or dearer to me. If a person treated me nicely, they were as close and as dear to me, as the brother I never had.

Sis Edna, as my great aunt Edna was called by everyone who knew her, was as close and as dear to me as anyone I met doing her life time, or since her death. This is based purely on how she treated me and nothing else.

I have set my standard for keeping my word by the way my great aunt Edna kept her word to me. Both of my grandparents on my mother's side came from fairly large families. There was no shortage of aunts, great aunts, great great aunts and assorted cousins once removed and not removed. But when the crowd was thinned out based on who did what for me, good old great aunt Edna stood then, and stands now, right at the top.

I understand that in the maze of family relationships, other people had children they favored based upon required family duty and personal choice, but I have to call it the way I personally viewed it. I don't now, nor have I ever, considered myself special and deserving of exceptional unearned treatment. This is one reason I have always attempted to show a person who has been nice to me that by directing any amount of their life-energy towards making my life more enjoyable is appreciated, and that that life-energy directed towards me will be treated as an investment which must be returned with interest.

My aunt Edna lived long enough for me to at least begin to show her how much I appreciated the things she had done for me as a child. I am certain she understood how much I appreciated her efforts, and that I clearly understood she didn't have to do the things she sacrificed her time and her resources to make my life more pleasant.

Although most of my relatives lived to be one hundred years old or older, my Sis Edna was not one of this group, she died in her late seventies. I am certain she would have lived much longer, if her husband of over fifty years had not predeceased her.

Through aunt Edna's kindnesses, I learned to only say what I mean, mean what I say and do what I promise to do, exactly when I promise to do it. Of all of the relatives on my mother's side of the family, each an excellent person, my aunt Edna was the safe port in the storm. She always did exactly what she told me she was going to do, as she promised to do it and like clock-work, she delivered on time.

In the late 1940s, after WWII, things were tough in our Southern county. Getting stuff out of the stores was really difficult. There wasn't much in the stores to get, even if you had the means. So, growing what you ate, making what you wore , and building the house you lived-in was mandatory.

We were a stable family and wanting for necessities was not in the picture. What made life special for me during my early years were the small touches that exceed the necessities. I never wanted for food, clothes or a warm bed. However, I always wanted something more, and the something-more came from my great aunt Edna. During my developmental years my aunt Edna was a magician in the kitchen and could turn basic staples into culinary treats of international quality and delight. This is all the more important for me now, as I look back, I realize that, if my aunt Edna was not dirt poor, she was doing a good job of creating the illusion. Not that being poor, or appearing to be poor when you were not, was uncommon in the county. The social ethic in the South at this time was to keep what you had in secret, and appear to be no-better off than was necessary.

If you had money, you spent it sparingly. If you did not have money, you did not complain about not having it. Children were told there were things they couldn't have, and ordered not to let it affect the enjoyment of their day.

Work was directly associated with getting things you wanted or needed. Deferring acquisitions until you had worked and made the money was the rule. This is why I can't say my aunt Edna was actually poor. I don't know how financially well off she and my maternal grandmother's youngest brother, her husband, were.

I do know they owned their own little farm, but they lived in a house that was so small the closet where they hung their Sunday clothes was about the same size as the bed room they slept in. The bed room was so close to the kitchen, you only had to take a few steps to get to the wood burning stove where Sis Edna baked those delicious cakes, cookies and pies.

None of this, however, was important to me, or to anyone else in the county who knew my great aunt Edna. She was a warm and friendly woman, and she always greeted everyone with a smile and instantly offered me whatever I wanted, or that she thought I could use from whatever she had or was expecting to get.

Even if you had money, using as little of it as possible was the watchword of the times. I always marveled at the way my Sis Edna went into her kitchen and make some of the best desserts. As I have indicated, getting stuff out of the stores was no easy task. I am still trying to figure out now, some seven decades later, just how she did what she did with so little to do it with.

My all-time favorite dessert was great aunt Edna's jelly cake. I knew that she made the jelly from the wild berries growing on the fence on the edge of the woods. I now realized, that she either grew, canned or prepared by hand, everything that she made for me.

Looking back at my childhood years sitting by the wood burning tin heater in the corner of their little house, I realize the importance of making due with what you have produced yourself and also sharing what you have with others.

During this pandemic, many decades after my childhood, my knowledge, and thus my understanding of what was happening right before my eyes in this small Southern county, comes into very clear focus. Co-existing with apartheid-like racism, poverty and a general state of societal economic decline and still attempting to create an atmosphere of

love, joy and giving to someone you didn't have to be nice to, was a miracle of
uncommon proportions. I have been
blessed to have seen and have been a
beneficiary these miracles.

If Southern Baptist had saints, I
would submit my Great Aunt Edna's
name for canonization. Her true miracles were creating special things out of
nothing, delivering them to others with
an open heart, and having my heart light
up over seven decades later during a
worldwide health crisis just by thinking
of her. Witnessing these miracles in
times worst than this pandemic assures
me I can and I will not only make it
through, but come out better on the other
side.

Even though after I became an
adult I continually attempted to show my
Sis Edna how much I appreciated her
demonstrated love for me, she did not
live long enough for me to pay her back
fully. During this pandemic, I certainly
have plenty of opportunity to do what
my great aunt Edna did for me for others.

What distinguished my Sis Edna
from other people in my life was her
unique ability to not only share with me
without restrictions everything that she

had, but her ability to unwaveringly do this when she said she was going to do it.

When I would see my Sis Edna at church service, she would come over to me and say, " . . . Junior, I am going to bake you some sweet bread and a jelly cake next Friday." Well, I could buy the ice cream on Thursday night or early Friday morning. The cake and the sweet bread were always delivered when and as promised.

I don't believe I ever told my Sis Edna she was the reason I always keep my word. I know I did tell her I would never forget her kindnesses to me. I did get many opportunities to do things for her and share my financial achievements with her long before she died. But looking back in the isolation of this pandemic, I really don't believe I ever got around to just sitting down with her and telling her exactly why I loved her so much. Now that she is dead, I have to just assume she knew. I have to think she was smart enough to know who she was creating when she spent her time with me. After all, even I finally realized that her objective was to teach me by example. Sitting here, breathing through a mask, and wearing a plastic

shield, I understand she was preparing
me to deal with things she had already
faced.

Over the years since I sat and
learned at the feet of my great aunt
Edna, I have done things for others I did-
n't want to do, when I didn't want to do
them, but understanding the people
needed them and needed them then.
Many times those people didn't thank
me or appreciate my efforts, but I have
always thanked my great aunt Edna for
teaching me I needed to be there and re-
spond when needed.

I guess, hell I know, I can say everything I need to know to make it through
this pandemic, I learned from my great
aunt Edna. I always called her Sis Edna,
because everyone else in the county did,
but for me, she will always be a very
special Great Aunt.

CHAPTER TW0

UNCLE LITTLE BUDDY

UNCLE LITTLE BUDDY

My mother's youngest brother was a small man by country farm standards. He stood only about five feet seven inches tall. At his heaviest weight he was only about 140 pounds fully clothed in the two plaid shirts he wore in both summer and winter.

Because he was so small in stature, and his oldest brother was also of substantially more girth, my mother's youngest brother was called Little Buddy. The name was not only appropriate, because of his diminutive size, but because his only male sibling was called Buddy. Nick names in the county were unimaginative, but descriptive.

Over time I came to learn Buddy was a nick name typically assigned to boys in farm families in the 1920s and

30s. So, among my uncles, I was privi-
leged to have an uncle Little Buddy and
an uncle Big Buddy.

My mother's youngest brother,
Little Buddy, was the knee baby of his
family. He had one sister younger than
he was, but she was larger in stature.

Little Buddy's signature trait was
his wide smile. Most folks in the county
called it a grin, because whenever you
saw Little Buddy, you always saw all of
his pearly white teeth. His perfectly
round head was about the size of a
grown man's two fists held together. He
always exhibited a close hair cut that allowed you to see every vane that led up-
wards from his neck and disappeared
close to the top of his head.

Although Little Buddy was about
two-thirds the size of a typical farm
hand, he was as strong as an ox, and
could do the physical work of any two
men and a small boy.

Following in his father's footsteps, my maternal grandfather, which he
did literally every day, Little Buddy

gained a reputation for being a reliable hard-worker who did precisely what his father told him to do, when his father told him to do it. This was good and bad. It was good because when Little Buddy's father, my maternal grandfather, told you to do something, he didn't want to discuss it. My grandfather wanted you to do what he told you to do promptly without question. Fortunately, he was a mastermind and tended to always be right.

Little Buddy's unique ability to do what his father told him to do was bad, because there was no other employment with that particular job description for him to move on to, if his father ever passed. This did not present a realistic problem, since all of our relatives tended to live and work until their 100th birthday, unless they died earlier.

My uncle Little Buddy, as was the custom with young unmarried adult males in rural farm families, worked 12 to 14 hours per day. Stopped early only on Saturdays.

On Saturdays the farm boys across the county would get together, get in their new cars, dapper dress casual clothes and start looking for girls. Early Sunday morning, they would all come home, get a few hours of sleep, get suited-up and head for church, whether they wanted to go or not.

Little Buddy was not a complex person. His trade mark method of talking, which he incessantly employed, was to pose a question to you and ask " . . .how can they do that . . . is it legal?" No matter what your response, he would always take the opposite side, and the conversation would never end.

As I matured and became old enough to act like I was a fully-growed man, about the time of my 9th or 10th birthday, I was assigned to my uncle Little Buddy as his helper, both before and after school. Before school, because there was always a long list of chores to be performed before the school bus came at about 7:30 a.m. And, after school, a full days work also had to be completed.

Working with my uncle Little Buddy was my inspiration for wanting to get a college education. During the long days and even longer years from the time I was old enough to drive a tractor, I watched my uncle Little Buddy walk in his father's footsteps, and I walked in his.

I did not have to be told to study and get good grades. I realized early on that if I didn't go to college and remained on the farm, I would always have to take orders from my elders, or at least until the day I got my own farm. I had a great deal of respect for my seniors, but I didn't want to become one of them.

Without a doubt, my uncle Little Buddy was the hardest working man I have ever met or heard of. During my 18 and three-quarter years of living on the farm, and the 50 years or so since I left, I have not met anyone, male or female, with my uncle's ability to constantly work hard and produce desired results. I now, dealing with this pandemic, truly respect and continue to admire this man.

As time has passed, I have come to appreciate having been in a position during my developmental stages, where someone else made the important decisions as I watched, kept quiet and learned. What a relief it would be now to have an elder deal with the continued downs of this crona virus. Now that I run my own business and must adapt and re-adapt as the worldwide health crisis progresses, I am even more impressed with my ancestors' ability to day-after-day make something out of nothing.

As a result of working in the fields with my uncle Little Buddy up until I graduated high school, I grew physically taller and larger than he was. I am certain that some, but not all, of his strengths rubbed off on me. I never did learn to follow the instructions of my superiors and seniors, and like it. But I did learn to do so and not show that I didn't like it. I am not bragging about this though, because I have come to understand that the responsibilities of leadership are many, and in most instances not desired.

I have been buttressed during the last 10 months of dealing with this pandemic by thinking of my early development on the farm under the watchful-stern eyes of my elders. At the time I didn't realize they had been through exactly what I am going through now, nor did I realize they were preparing me to survive when it was my time to sit in the hot seat and lead.

I managed to get through college and I never spend more than two consecutive days on the farm again. I did visit several times a year, and during those brief visits, my uncle Little Buddy and I talked and laughed about my efforts to get from under his supervision. There have been many times since I became my own man when I really wanted to retreat to the safe-lock-step existence of farm life, but I never admitted it to my uncle Little Buddy. I have learned that following in lock step as ordered is also a tenant of successful professional employment.

The passage of time, participation in a foreign war, and several career changes have caused me to look back on my farm days with warmth, particularly now when the economic down turn requires working longer hours, accepting more responsibility, and doing things I really don't want to do.

Today some of my favorite memories are of following my uncle Little Buddy's footsteps through the fields as he followed his father's, my grandfather's orders to the letter.

As uncle Little Buddy got older his father, my grandfather, passed. It became necessary for him to lead and not follow. Unfortunately, my grandfather broke the family tradition and did not live to be 100 years old. He passed at 90.

I never spend much time with my uncle Little Buddy after his father's death. The little time I did spend with

him gave me great hope for his successful survival. He no longer farmed. Tobacco was no longer a good cash crop
and cotton was no longer king. Industry
had come to the county, my uncle found
a factory job and not only survived, but
became a model employee. As it turned
out, the ability to work hard, follow instructions without question and work a 6
day week with frequent over-time was
exactly what factory employers were
looking for.

My uncle Little Buddy didn't enjoy an overly long life by family standards. He died in his early seventies. The
family still talks about his ability to end-
lessly hold conversations and say nothing with great enthusiasm and zeal,
about his small round head, tough coun-
tenance and the way he was his father's,
my grandfather's, shadow. He, and his
father are together again now. Neither
one of them probably wants to farm any
more, at least I hope not, because if they
do, when I join them, I will again hold
the low slot. I hope God knows I don't

want to farm any more either. I am
thankful, however, that growing up on
the farm has equipped me to work
through this pandemic.

CHAPTER THREE

BROTHER FRED

BROTHER FRED

In the early 1950s on Sundays after church we had a family tradition. Everyone gathered at my grandfather's house and sat around from about 2:00 p.m. until dark. This was a year around phenomena and the length of the sessions varied from about two hours in the fall and winter to a little more than three hours in the spring and summer.

We were a farm community and work was based upon the number of hours you could see without turning the lights on, not by a predetermined hypothetical schedule. Lighting was a significant factor in the rural South in the late 1940s and early 50s. This was the period after World War II, the country was modernizing and in rural areas getting

electricity to every house was more important than getting every dirt road
paved. Outside toilets were standard and
recycling newspapers didn't mean stack-
ing them on a curb for once per week
pick-up.

I remember these times as not being
easy or pleasant by standards then or
now. These are the earliest of my memories, and the things that have changed
the most because of technology really
stand out in my mind. There was no tel-
evision outside of the major metropoli-
tan cities, the only telephone in the
county was at the gas station on the main
high way, and a wood burning fire place
was not a decorative accent.

I remember coming in from the
fields in the evenings, washing up, eating and sitting in front of our tall-cabinet
radio. One of the adults always turned
from station to station as the signal faded
in and out. The radio had a long wire
antenna that ran out of the window and
up the side of the house. Even with the
antenna, the signal was always weak and

the stations mostly had only country music.

My mother and I lived with her father and mother. From what I managed to piece together, we came to live with my grandparents after my mother and father separated. This must have been when I was two or three years old. I have absolutely no memory of this, and I can literally remember pretty much everything that happened to me after I was about four years old.

According to family legend, my mother met my father when he was a young service man and one of the first blacks to join the Marine corps after the presidential order lifting the racial barrier.

As my paternal grandmother relates it, she found out that my father had joined the Marines after she had sent his tuition check to Tuskegee. She only talked to me about this once in a passing conversation. I must have been 15 or 16 years old and we were talking on one of my Christmas visits. After that, I never inquired and no additional details were ever provided.

I understand that when my mother and father met, my mother was fresh out of college and was teaching high school. My father had dropped out of college to be in the first group of blacks to join the Marines. From what I was told over time by various family members, neighbors and unofficial community historians, when my father got out of the Marines we moved up North to his home town. Apparently, the marriage went downhill from there. My father couldn't live in the South and would not accept a janitorial job in the North. My mother would work anywhere, but would not settle for living with her in-laws. They went their separate ways and I came back South with my mother.

I only remember having one conversation with my mother about the marriage and that was the day the divorce papers arrived. I was about four years old. I remember mother sitting me down and telling me "... your father and I are not going to live together any more. It has nothing to do with you. He is a good person, I am a good person, but we can't live together. It has nothing to do with you." She asked me if I understood, I said yes, and the conversation was over. We never discussed the matter again over the next 50 or so years.

I do recall thinking to myself, " . . . why would she think I would believe that it was about me, I didn't put them together?" I also recall thinking, ". . . . this is great, now I won't have to be bothered that much." Even as a young child, I valued my privacy, and the less people said to me, the better.

I never really cared that my mother and father were divorced, and never sought an explanation from my mother, father or other relatives. I do remember my mother saying from time to time that she would never get married again. After my own divorce, I knew why my parents didn't stay together, and I also learned why I should have never gotten married myself.

Well, back down South, I became the apple of my maternal grandmother's eye. Her philosophy was " . . . idle hands are the devil's workshop."

The grand parents in a farm family were in charge of instilling in the grandchildren the work ethic that was mandatory for survival in an agricultural community. I can remember from an early age being taught playing ball, sitting on the front porch watching the occasional car pass-by, and talking unnecessarily to neighbors about things that were none of my business was taboo.

Prior to entering the first grade, I had to get up each morning and go to the fields with whomever was going to feed the draft animals and livestock. If I was too small to work in the fields, I had to go and watch those who could work, or go back and forth to the field hand water pump and bring fresh water in a clear glass gallon pickle-jar.

The way we lived six of the seven days of the week was simple and consistent. It involved getting up no later than 5 a.m., getting dressed, eating a hardy breakfast and being in the fields before the dew dried at sun rise.

My maternal grandfather was a legend in the county for being an early riser and for getting all of his children up and out with him. People would say, " . . . if you want to see Mr. Wilson, you better be standing in his yard before the sun comes up." Everyone knew that, if you wanted to do business with my grandfather, you either talked with him before he left home in the morning, or you came and worked beside him as he worked. He would not stop work to talk with anyone about anything, and you could not watch him and talk to him without pitching in. There were no exceptions.

I tell you all of this, because it puts into perspective how important Sunday evenings were for me. On Sunday mornings, I had to go to Sunday school and then to church. I could pick any of the local churches, my folks didn't press any one religion. County churches at the

time ran for several hours. Starting
11:30 a.m. or so., services typically
lasted until about 2 p.m. or longer.

Church was about the main social ac-
tivity in our southern farm community,
and even if you were not particularly re-
ligious, you went for the association, the
meals after service, and for me, to meet
girls.

The high point of my Sunday was
waiting for my relatives to come over after church to relax a few hours. I was
never a part of the conversation on these
occasions, because the rule was " . . .
children were to be seen and not heard."
There was a definite pecking order, the
older people were at the top and children
at the bottom.

I came to learn this strict rule was
based on the difficulty of surviving in
the rural South doing segregation. People would say, " . . . you don't get old by
being a fool and you don't know anything until you are old." Many, many
years later, I fully understand what the
old folks meant. Speaking without

knowledge is the most dangerous form of free speech.

On those Sunday evenings, I got to sit and listen to my elders, and I learned why they did what they did, and how they suffered the injustices of racism that society had thrust upon them. Looking back there were certain things, I now realize I wasn't suppose to hear and probably somethings, I wasn't suppose to see.

Drinking alcohol and playing cards was forbidden in my grandfather's house. We lived in a dry county and to get alcohol it was necessary to drive to the next county, or get it from a local boot legger. No matter how old my seniors were, when my grandfather pulled into the yard, the cards were hidden and the drinks were carefully put under the sofa until he passed through.

Bootleg liquor was the cocaine of the 1940s and 50s. Not as destructive as cocaine today, but just as hidden by users, and just as sought after by law enforcement.

I gradually understood my elders had

figured out a way of dispatching me during the only hours each week they had to talk about adult matters, drink a little bootleg liquor and play cards.

My maternal grandmother's youngest brother was named Fred. He was a tall slim man with a high forehead and a receding hair line. He chewed tobacco constantly and waived his hands in an instructive manner like a college professor when he talked. He had no children and he and my mother were best friends. He adopted me as his own and spend every moment he could being like a father to me.

The first and only circus I recall attending was with my great uncle Fred and his wife. They showed me my first live elephant, got me the first hot dog I remember eating away from home, and the only cotton candy I have ever eaten. This was, and continues to be over seventy years later, one of the high points in my life.

After Sunday services, my grandfather was at the church discussing church

business with the minister, my grandmother was over visiting her oldest sister, and my aunts and uncles had the
evening to be, what I now know was
their only time to be independent adults.

I was the oldest grandchild and I
couldn't be allowed to see young adults
drink beer or play cards. My great uncle
Fred figured out a way to get rid of me
for an hour or so while adults did their
thing. He would give me a quarter
(about $5.00 now). At this time male
farm hands earned fifty cents per hour.
With this quarter, I could go to the local
store, get a soda, a few two for a penny
Commodore cookies, some grapes, a two
cent Baby Ruth and have change left to
spend during the next week.

Time and adult experiences have
taught me, not only how hard great uncle
Fred had to work for that quarter, but
how much it meant for me to receive it.
Thanks to great uncle Fred giving me
those quarters, I never did learn to drink
alcohol or to play cards. Sitting here doing this pandemic, I can designate every

quarter to life's necessities, and even if I am tempted to waste money on drinking or gambling, I just don't know how to do so.

Prior to his death, I took every opportunity I could to let him know I appreciated the things he had done for me and the example he had set. I would give him $25.00 when I saw him and tell him I knew it was less than the twenty-five cents he had given me thirty years earlier. I still miss that man, what I wouldn't give to have him ride out this corona virus thing with me. He died in his late seventies or early eighties, but he gave me over a hundred years of joyful memories.

CHAPTER FOUR

BROTHER DUCK

BROTHER DUCK

As I sit here trying to figure out what I have to do to make it through this pandemic, the faces and voices of my long deceased relatives and friends come to me. Sometimes they speak, sometimes they just give me a knowing-smile. At other instances, they are just working in the fields waiving for me to come join them.

My second cousin was a man that everyone in the county called Duck. He was my maternal grandfather's youngest sister's child. I never met my grandfather's youngest sister. She died before I was born. I understand that she died giving birth to the man everyone called Duck.

I don't remember the name of my grandfather's youngest sister now, nor do I recall whether I ever knew it. From what I have been able to piece together, she passed on about 1912 or so. I base this on the age of her only son relative to my mother's age. Duck and my mother were close friends. My mother was six years younger than her first cousin Duck.

Although I did not get to meet my second cousin Duck's mother, I did get to know well his father. When I first remember him, my deceased great aunt's husband was in his late seventies or early eighties. He was the sharpest dressing man in the county. He was never seen not wearing a white shirt, tie, well pressed pants and mirror-shined shoes. This is significant, because there were no white-collar jobs for blacks in the county.

No one in the county ever talked about Duck's father ever having a job or doing any kind of manual labor. This was rare in a farming community, you either owned your own farm, share-cropped or worked for someone who either owned a farm or share-cropped.

Ducks father was the exception. When I say that no one ever mentioned

Duck's father's name in the same sentence as the word "work", this includes his own brother-in-law, my grandfather, whose youngest sister was Duck's father's first wife.

Not a single soul in the county professed to know exactly how old Duck's father actually was, and this includes Duck himself. My grandfather could only say Duck's father was a middle age man, when he dated and married his youngest sister.

My grandfather said it was not known how Duck's father supported himself and his family, but he did. There was no crime in our county, so however he did it, it was legal. I never figured it out, but that is probably because by the time I developed the ability to reason, Duck's father was already way passed retirement age.

As the story was relayed to me over the more than 40 year period that I either lived in the county or visited often on holidays, my own relatives and others, told the story of how Duck's father remarried within a respectable period, but not long after his wife, my grandfather's youngest sister, died. After all, he had a young son to care for. This was around the turn of the century and in our small farming community, there was no such thing as day care.

Duck, my second cousin on my mother's side, survived to become the senior sibling of a family of about five or six children. He was raised by his father's second wife, a quiet dutiful woman named Jane.

My second cousin Duck told me over the years, " . . . Miss Jane, as his step mother was called, treated me as if I were her own son." In fact, my second cousin Duck's children, never having known their own grandmother, my grandfather's deceased baby sister, believed with all of their hearts, that Miss Jane was their real grandmother. Distinctions were only made between the oldest boy Duck, and the rest of the children, when there was a discussion of work habits.

Duck was known as the hardest worker. People would say, if Duck was not working, he was planning on going to work. Don't misunderstand me, they were all industrious boys, well almost all with the exception of the baby boy, but there was something about Duck with respect to work, that distinguished him, not only from his younger siblings, but from just about anyone else in the county.

Duck worked harder and accomplished more during the work day than almost anyone. Having worked with Duck on his farm makes anything I have to do today to make it through this pandemic seem minor.

My mother told me her first cousin Duck was never really known by his real name, but from childhood was known as Duck. As the story went, the community boys got together after a hard week's work and would go over to a local farmer's poultry farm and take a duck to roast in the woods over an open fire. Keep in mind this was long before

TV and even readily available radio broadcasts. It was around 1920 or so and taking a duck from a poultry farm with thousands of birds wasn't considered a real crime.

Legend has it that Duck got his name by being the best at getting into the poultry houses quickly, grabbing a bird and running away without getting caught. The name "Duck" stuck with him until his death at age 91. His grave marker includes his real name, but in quotes, his only used name, "Duck".

Duck's father lived until the early 1970s and was by all accounts over 100 years old. It was not possible to tell his age by looking at him, with his tight dark skin, always bald head and wrinkle free face. At his death, if Duck's father did not have every one of his own teeth, the ones he did have were a great credit to a dentist technically far ahead of his profession.

Calculating today on how to work to succeed through the remainder

of 2020 and go into next year successfully, I realize I have seen my people
survive the hardest of times by using
both pure hard work and mental acumen.
I understand hard times have been just
standard times most of my life, and that
during the life of my ancestors, what is
happening now is just regular life.

Between my maternal second
cousin Duck and his father, I have the
knowledge and experience to work and
think my way through Covid-19 and
prosper. Even though they are gone,
they keep coming back to me, letting me
know they are available for consultation.
Anyway, the entire point here is to tell
you how my second cousin Duck, my
maternal grandfather's youngest sister's
only son and his father have contributed
to the knowledge I need to get up each
morning and beat the negative social and
economic effects of Covid-19. Because
they grew up, survived and prospered
during worst times for people like me
than this, I have no excuses. Their strong

positive examples have helped me for-
mulate my own goals.

I continue to reflect and think
fondly of the hot days and long nights I
worked with my second cousin Duck on
his farm. Listening to his motivational
speeches on the benefits of hard honest
work and the rewards of being his own
boss were like college economic lec-
tures.

He taught me that being your
own boss means you can never complain
about the quality of the leadership, that
your pay days are totally dependent on
whether you did work that was productive, and that there were no vacation
days.

I never fully adopted his philosophy, but I am certainly reviewing it now
to see what I shouldn't have excluded.
Hard times like these make me look
back to determine my forward direction.
There are some days that make me wish
I was back on the farm following in lock
step with my ancestors who were wiser
and stronger than I am, but I understand

that my wise ancestors are gone now.

    Thank God they lived to be 100 years old, or died only slightly earlier, and shared their secrets with me.

CHAPTER FIVE

JACKSON NEVER HAD A FIRST NAME

JACKSON NEVER HAD A FIRST NAME

Five friends of mine have died since March of this year, none from Covid-19. Each day I wrestle with them being gone, and how the circle of my childhood friends has now become just a few dots connected by a straight line.

Over the years as my senior family members and friends have elected to accept their eternal rewards, the strangest mental feeling I have experienced has been wanting to sit down with them and discuss how I felt about them moving on and leaving me here. Strangely, first I feel anger over my selfish-cherished loved-ones just leaving me without even a I-don't-want-to-go-but-I-have-to-move-on. Then I come to my senses and accept the fact they didn't want to go, but had no choice. I have lost so many of those that I have depended on to help me make it through my day, I no longer grieve or cry, I just accept the fact they are gone, and I will sit down with them in the Spirit World at some point and discuss with them my personal hurt over them leaving me at the most difficult times in my life.

Reflecting during these long days of isolation, I can recall the first time that I experienced the desire to sit down and discuss the death of a departed friend with that friend.

In the late 1970s I lived on the corner of 4th and Angela Street in the South East section of town. It was my practice at the time to get my hair cut every other week, whether it needed it or not. A 2 block walk from my little row house, there was a three chair barber shop owned and operated by a man named Jackson.

Strangest thing, I never really knew Jackson's first name and never thought it important to ask. Over the years he cut my hair with precision, and precisely every two weeks as was the custom, Jackson and I had become good friends.

I never ever saw him outside of his barber shop, never saw him without his hard-starched white barber's jacket, and never learn where he lived. I did know Jackson was a man with unwavering work habits. Not only was he the best barber I have ever had, he was the most reliable.

I could always count on Jackson to be there when I needed to get my hair cut, and this in itself gains significance, when I tell you I always got my hair cut at 6:30 a.m. The day of the week would vary between Tuesday and Thursday, but the time was pretty much always the same. The time was based on my farm upbringing. Back in the South on my grandfather's farm, the sun never found us in bed and 50 plus years later, after I have lived in several different cities and many different countries, the early rising habit still remains.

Anyway, back to Jackson and my desire to discuss with him his own death.

I had formed a bond with Jackson based upon, not only his ability to cut my hair the way that I thought the girls liked it, but also because we were both morning people who believed that providing a predictable professional service with skill was what life was all about.

I first found Jackson's Barber Shop as I was standing on the corner waiting for a city bus to take me down town to my job. I was going to graduate school at night at the time. I would get up at about 4 a.m., study a few hours, get dressed and head to work a few hours before the office opened. This meant I could get some more studying done before work started.

One morning I noticed Jackson sitting in the window of the barber shop looking back at me. I assumed that this man was a barber and pointed to my head. Jackson nodded, waived his hand,

and I headed in. The man read my mind.
He got up and with one continuous mo-
tion opened the locked door and the clip-
pers started.

During this period in the 70s, I
had little time for personal excesses like
taking time during the day to get my hair
cut. Working a fulltime job and going to
night graduate school pretty much consumed all of my time.

As I entered the shop Jackson
turned on the lights, greeted me as if we
had known each other all of our lives,
and asked me how I wanted my hair cut.
I told him that morning and he never inquired again. He always cut it right,
never a hair out of place, and with my
hair that was truly no easy task.

From that morning Jackson became my barber, confident, philosophi-
cal collaborator and spiritual friend. He
remains so until this day, now over forty
years after his death. This is strange, especially since, I never ever saw or inter-
acted with Jackson outside of his barber
shop. But doing our bi-weekly contacts

we grew to know each other's personal and private thoughts.

I never knew Jackson's wife, although I knew he had one. I knew that she was a woman he loved very much, but a woman totally unlike him in her approach to life and work. He told me she was always asleep when he left home in the early morning hours to drive across town to his shop, that she had spending habits which consumed all of her personal income, and that he didn't mind, because she was the joy of his life. I grew to think that since I knew Jackson and he was my friend, his wife was my friend also.

It never occurred to me during our early morning sessions my friend Jackson and I would ever end the morning talks and hair adjustments. He was a young robust man of about 45 years, he never complained about the weather, his health, the long work hours or anything else. It never occurred to me I would have to one day find a new Jackson, because Jackson was the perfect barber and friend.

Over the years Jackson was so regular, if I passed his shop, and he was not sitting in his chair with the lights out so I could waive at him, I automatically knew it was a Monday, the only day the shop was closed.

Every day was the same for me at this time, work all day, study all night and waive at Jackson each morning except Mondays.

Well, one day, I can't remember any longer which day of the week, but I remember it was not a Monday, I walked up to the shop, didn't even look in and stood at the door waiting for Jackson to get up and open it. This had become a truly unique and meaningful ritual for me. I didn't hold a routine unique and special relationship with many people at this time, and I certainly appreciated this one. I always knew once I appeared, Jackson would get up and open the door for me. When this didn't happen and the lights didn't come on, I did a visual search and didn't see Jackson. I turned around, looked across the street and didn't see his 7 year old yellow Mercury with the black leather top. My first thought was it just had to be a Monday.

I took the bus to work believing it was a Monday. Because, over the years Jackson transformed himself from my barber into my friend who cut my hair, I had been able to set my calendar and clock by Jackson Time, always reliable, always punctual and always there for me when I needed him.

The following morning I knew the day before hadn't been a Monday. I again stood looking in the window of Jackson's Barber Shop, I didn't see Jackson. I realized that something was wrong and said to myself jokingly, " . . . if Jackson isn't here, he must be dead." In my heart I hoped I was wrong, but in my mind I knew it to be true.

As I stood there looking into the empty barber shop, I felt a certain lost. I somehow knew a major change had just occurred in my life. I didn't want to turn around, I didn't want to move, because I felt if I kept looking in the window, I would see Jackson. I also knew if I turned around, I would never see Jackson or his yellow Mercury again.

As I stood there, the silence was broken with a voice I recognized. Over the years Jackson had been my barber our early morning relationship had grown to include one other person. As my hair was being cut prior to the shop officially opening, a little old lady, who must have been in her eighties or nineties, would walk up, tap on the window and greet us. Jackson would always say something pleasant to her, and we would all smile, and then act as if our lives had been enriched.

That morning before I turned around the old lady said, " . . . son, you are waiting for Jackson, Jackson is dead."

By the time I turned around to look at her, she had walked up the block. She looked back and added, " . . . Jackson had a heart attack." She walked off, I took the bus to work. I never saw her again, and if I did see her, I just didn't recognize her. We were both creatures of habit, so we must have seen each other again, I just didn't recognize her without Jackson.

I came to realize not only how much my relationship with Jackson meant to me, but how very, very little I knew about the man I cherished as a friend. For the next several days I wanted to call Jackson's wife and tell her who I was, tell her I certainly knew her through her husband, but I didn't know where to call. I never knew Jackson's first name and while writing this piece, I also realize Jackson didn't know my last name. We were friends of the heart. I couldn't call his wife and tell her I truly shared her loss, nor could I attend the funeral and pay my last respects. Jackson was just gone.

Weeks later, as I walked pass Jackson's shop, I said to myself, " . . . I can't wait to sit down with Jackson and tell him how our little old lady told me about his death. I am going to tell him how I realized he must have been dead, when I didn't see him for two days and didn't see his 7 year old yellow Mercury parked across the street." I thought to myself I will tell Jackson how much he was a part of my life, then it hit me, Jackson was gone and if I hadn't communicated to him the power and strength of our nameless relationship, I couldn't do so then.

Three of my friends have heard my Jackson story, none of them knew Jackson, and now all three of them are dead. I hope my deceased friends tell Jackson what I never told him, when they meet on the other side.

Since Jackson's death, I have tried on a regular basis to let my friends know what they mean to me. Reflecting during this pandemic, I did demonstrate to my five friends who have died since March what they meant to me and the positive effects they had on my life. Now when I meet them on the other side, I will only have to tell them how upset I was when they died and left me here to face Covid-19 alone.

CHAPTER SIX

MY COUSIN MARIE

MY COUSIN MARIE

My mother's first cousin Marie had a voice that made Aretha Franklin sound like an amateur. I think my maternal second cousin Marie is still alive, but I am not sure. I rarely got to see her after I left the farm, because Marie never came out much, at least if she did, I didn't see her.

I think she got married right after she graduated high school, but again, I am not sure. I never remember seeing her with a husband and I never remember her having children, though I think she got married and had several. What I do remember and what I know for sure is that, if anybody in the county died, cousin Marie always sang the last solo sending them to the next world.

Marie had the voice of an angel.

The only thing that kept her from becoming a world-famous singer was her inability to stay outside of her mother's house for more than the time needed to sing at funerals and church services.

After I left home and traveled, Marie would often come to my mind when I realized in comparison to the professional singers I had occasion to hear, Marie had treated me to the voice of a premiere diva at weekly church services.

As I sat with friends after musicals on Broad Way, I would tell them about my mother's first cousin Marie, my maternal grandmother's oldest sister's only daughter. I would say, " . . . you know, my mother had a cousin who sings so much better than that." I doubt anyone actually believed me, but it always made for a good after theater conversation.

It is amazing how you can go to any small country church in the South on a Sunday morning, and if you can manage to sit through an hour and a half or better of a spirit-filled-divinely-call-representative of the Cross, you can finally hear a solo by a voice, but for location and fancy staging, rivals any you will hear on any professional concert stage anywhere in the world. I call this my "equal distribution per small country church soloist theory."

Having lived in Georgia, North Carolina, Arkansan, Mississippi and Louisianian, I can say, based on experience, you will never attend a small church service and not hear a member of the choir who couldn't hold his or her own anywhere in the world. I often wonder what made an Aretha Franklin and what made a cousin Marie. Well, I have heard the Aretha Franklin story second hand, but I know the cousin Marie story first hand.

When I was growing up, I got to see cousin Marie at funerals mostly. We attended different churches for regular services. Although Marie was my grandmother's sister's child and we lived in the same county not more than five country miles apart, we didn't do much visiting. In a farming community in the old South, after a day's work in the fields, there wasn't much socializing.

As I recall, one of the reasons we didn't do much visiting is my grandmother's sister lived about a country mile off of the main paved road at the end of a one lane dirt path. Only three people lived in the house. There was my mother's cousin Marie, her father, and my grandmother's oldest sister.

I recall going with my grandfather to pick up my grandmother one Sunday after church, and wondering if we would ever drive through the long unpaved country road. I was very small and dating the time by the 1950 Chevy my grandfather was driving, I imagine that it was early 1950 or late 1949. This was the last time I remember going all the way up to my cousin Marie's house. I must have gone back there at least once more, it was another fourteen or so years before I grew up and left the county. I, just for the life of me, at this time, over sixty years later, never remember going up there again.

I remember standing on the front bench seat of my grandfather's car long before safety belts, and wondering if we would ever drive through the long dirt road and reach the large clearing in the piney woods where the house with the 3 person pouch stood.

On this particular Sunday in the middle of the summer, it had been raining for a couple of days. After turning off the high way, the dirt road that had been cut through the trees was muddy and slippery. The narrowness of the road, the un-timelessness of meeting another car coming towards us, reinforces my memory of this particular Sunday.

In a county filled with narrow, barely more than one way dirt roads, there was a rule experienced drivers followed, and little boys standing on the front seat of their grandfather's cars soon learned. If you are on a narrow dirt road, as soon as you see another car coming, pull to the side and stop. This was more than southern dirt road courtesy, it was a basic rule of survival.

On a dirt road, particularly on a rainy day, the first person to stop forced the other driver to go around. The quickest to stop, became the driver who either, went to get help for the driver slow to stop who slid into the ditch, or had the pleasure of providing assistance in getting the car out of the ditch. There was no AAA. There were few telephones, none of them mobile, and the few phones were mostly at the local gas stations.

On this particular Sunday, my grandfather was the first to stop, and we were pleased with the opportunity to assist the other driver to get out of the ditch. Sitting here doing this pandemic, I can't remember the identity of the other driver, but the situation comes to mind as I try to figure out how to maneuver through the unknown road ahead. Remembering how my grandfather always quickly adapted to any situation and came out ahead, thinking about the soothing tones of Marie's voice, I hear them both saying to me, " . . . keep going, you will make it."

After I graduated high school and left the county, I, from time to time, did return for funerals and holidays, but as tradition had it, I only saw Marie when I returned for funerals. As it had been before I grew up and left the farm, my grandmother's sister's only daughter Marie was always the final soloist. This was true whether she was related to the deceased or not.

It was hard for Marie not to be related to the deceased in our small county, either by marriage or blood. It wouldn't have mattered anyway, because with funerals, no one could send the deceased home like Marie.

In planning what to do in the worst economic down turn in American history, my flash backs center on how cousin Marie changed from the young woman she was when I first remember her to a fairly senior adult with graying hair. I am strengthened by the fact she made it during a time much more difficult than it is now. I have never had the opportunity to sit and talk with Marie and tell her how much I have talked and bragged about her over the years.

At my mother's funeral Marie sang the last solo, but by the time I thanked everyone for coming to pay their respects, Marie had gone. I did ask my uncle about her when I was home a few years ago. He told me Marie had gotten married and moved with her husband to the county seat. We talked about the fact Marie's voice had gotten better over the years. I learned she was still in demand at funerals, but still never sang commercially outside of the church. What a lost to the world, but I guess there already is an Aretha Franklin.

Doing this pandemic thoughts of death and avoiding it is a constant. In thinking how to avoid it, the cunning of my ancestors and the secrets they taught me gives me guidance and strength. I am no spring chicken now myself and

Marie is my senior.

I don't know whether I will go first or whether cousin Marie will predecease me, but if Marie out lives me, I would be real proud if she would sing the last solo for me.

CHAPTER SEVEN

MY OTHER AUNT GEORGIA

MY OTHER AUNT GEORGIA

I was blessed with two great aunts named Georgia. One was my maternal grandmother's sister. The other was my maternal grandfather's oldest sister.

As was the custom in my family, my grandfather's sister lived to be one hundred and two years old. At the time of her death, she looked exactly like her mother, who had died twenty or so years earlier at 103 years of age.

I really never got to know my great aunt Georgia, my grandfather's sister, very well. About the time I developed a memory and was old enough to walk independently around the neighborhood, she was already set in her ways. In the county this meant, she was so old she was not going to expand her list of significant others, and I was just a little low on the family tree for her to include me in her circle.

I remember my grandfather's senior sister was married to a man with the sur name Peters. I can't remember his first name for the life of me. I am certain I knew it at one time, but sitting here in isolation, social distancing, I am just failing to recall some details.

As I dig deeper into my memory bank, my grandfather's senior sister had retired from teaching school sometime in the mid to late 1940s. I recall she had several daughters who had also taught school, and at least one son who was a math teacher. I can only remember going over to my grandfather's senior sister's house on a few occasions. Her husband sold eggs and raised chickens. I can remember needing a fertilized egg to hatch for a second grade science project, and my mother had made arrangements for him to provide them.

I remember getting two eggs from him. One hatched and one didn't. That was the way the science project

was suppose to work. One egg was fertilized and one was not. It was probably
this project and the knowledge gained of
what the roster did to the egg to turn it
into a chicken that caused me to not like
eggs today. I never did have much for
eggs at breakfast after that project.

But, back to great aunt Georgia
on my grandfather's side of the family.
Besides remembering how she dupli-
cated her mother and lived to also be
over one hundred years old, I remember
her special project was tending to her
oldest daughter Carol. Carol needed
tending to because she could understand
reading, but she couldn't read writing.
In the county this meant although Carol
was smart enough not to walk out in
front of cars when she was crossing the
road, the better part of discretion meant
the family saw she didn't have the opportunity to cross the road often and
never alone.

My memories of my cousin Carol
and her mother, my paternal grandfather's senior sister, centers mostly around

them sitting on the rap-around porch on their big two-story red tar paper covered farm house. By the time I developed a memory, great aunt Georgia had retired and she and Carol always moved around the neighborhood together, and returned home together. Typically though, they sat motionless dead-center on the rap-around porch in the green and white steel swing sofa watching the cars go by.

I am sure they did things other than observe life pass by as they set on that porch, but I was too young to re-member anything else they did with the exception of weekly church attendance and weekly trips to the A&P grocery store in the next county. I do know around the time great aunt Georgia reached her 90th birthday talk in the fam-ily turned to who would tend to Carol af-ter her died. There was no urgency in these discussions, everyone knew great aunt Georgia would live another ten to fifteen years just like her mother did. It was the family custom, especially on my grandfather's side of the family, those who lived to be over ninety went into their own world slightly after 92 or 93, but would remain active through 100. Everyone was confident great aunt Georgia would be able to take care of herself and her daughter Carol for a long time.

As I look into the mirror during this pandemic, I observe my own hair turning an off shade of silver, I have also begun to look for, and hope I find, evidence of the family longevity gene. I take great pride in the fact my paternal grandfather's sister lived through the last pandemic and survived to be over 100 years old, and during times worst than these, but I am not sure I am as smart or as genetically well-endowed as she was.

I am now taking great solace in growing up working on the family farm, I was taught difficult times only make you stronger, and giving up is never an option.

When in the fields with adults and falling behind, they would always say, " . . . boy come on, what won't kill you, will make you stronger." Reflecting on growing up during a time when there were no industry or government jobs for black people, and survival required understanding you had to do more to get less, I have reason not to complain, or even consider current conditions a hindrance, but just a cause to grow stronger and prosper.

I don't remember what happened to cousin Carol after great aunt Georgia passed, but I am sure she was incorporated into the family structure and continued to be protected. It was the family way.

Now, living far from the county with all of my senior relatives deceased and the old family care system dissolved because all of the younger members have dispersed through the universe finding opportunities which did not exist 50 years ago, I draw strength from my ancestors and I am thankful I had them and face Covid-19 knowing I can beat it.

CHAPTER EIGHT

MY MATERNAL GRANDMOTHER'S OLDEST BROTHER

MY MATERNAL GRANDMOTHER'S
OLDEST BROTHER

For the life of me, I can't remember the name of my mother's mother's oldest brother. I do remember someone coming to our house early on a Sunday morning, I was about five years old, with news my grandmother's oldest brother had been killed in an automobile accident.

In a small town just north of us, a tractor trailer ran through a red light and hit my great uncle's car from behind killing him.

I remember it being a very sad time for my grandmother. She was always stern and never emotional, or out of control. My maternal grandmother was always the stable force in the family, and when she spoke, my mother and all

of her brothers and sisters stopped whatever they were doing, listened and did
whatever my grandmother told them to
do.

Everyone in the county apparently knew just how close my grandmother and her oldest brother were and
what a shock his death was for her. On
this day people came from near and far
to pay their respects, and to see what
they could do to comfort her.

My grandmother's brother lived
on a farm about two country miles from
our farm. As it comes back to me now, I
never really saw my great uncle except
on Sundays, and I also remember he was
always dressed in a very nice suit and
wore a gray felt hat with a black band.

I remember standing near his leg
and looking up at him, and then looking
down at his brown and white wing tip
shoes. I can't remember what his voice
sounded like, but I do remember he had
a wife named Mary and two children,
one boy and a very pretty girl who
looked exactly like her mother.

I remember my deceased great uncle's daughter was married and had a daughter who couldn't talk. The girl was born just before my great uncle's accidental death. I remember my grandmother talking about how her brother was doing everything he could to help his daughter and son-in-law manage.

My memory fails me as to whether I went to the funeral. I am not sure I went, but in the county at that time, when someone died, everyone in the family went to the funeral. One thing for sure, the Seas' Funeral Home buried him, they buried everyone in the family, whether they lived to be one hundred years old or not.

As I sit here intensely thinking about my ancestors and how they overcame difficult times like these, I can remember within a year or so after the funeral, my grandmother's brother's widow moved from the farm into town and was surrounded by family members who helped her adapt to the loss of her husband.

Family was always there in the old days to pick you up when you fell and needed help. There were no social services or government programs. Whatever happened you had to quickly get over it and move on.

I never remember anyone staying down long or taking time off from work to grieve. Life appeared to me, as a child, to be cold and deliberately cruel. I was taught to recognize this. I have come to understand over the years I was taught this, because it was true.

Long before the laws of discrimination were even considered anything but permanent, I never heard anyone say because they were black, there was something they couldn't do. I was always told, if you want to achieve something, just do it.

My grandmother was never the same after the death of her oldest brother. Now after having long lost my parents and all of my senior relatives, I understand why.

From listening to my mother and

her sisters talk, I for some reason think my maternal grandmother suffered an irreversible change that saddened her for the remainder of her life. Within a few years after the accident that killed my great uncle, my grandmother had the first of a series of strokes which eventually caused her death.

I was too young to make any connection to the death of her oldest brother to these strokes, and making that connection here and now during this pandemic, almost seventy years later, is probably not based on anything in reality.

Dealing with the rapid changes this pandemic is causing, I would like to pick up and return to the farm. My maternal grandmother isn't there so I can consult her. She didn't live to be 100 years old, as was the family custom. All of my senior relatives are now dead also. I am the oldest person in my family line. Now everyone calls me for the family history and advice.

It was a long time after my great

uncle's accidental death before another relative died. As close as I can remember, it was my grandmother who died next, then the family longevity gene kicked in. I must have been in high school before there was another family funeral.

After my grandmother's death, I planned for a short period on becoming an undertaker. For some reason in my child's mind, I believed that undertakers didn't died. I had never heard of anyone working in a funeral home dying. This was short lived, however, and when I learned that the family funeral director Mr. Seas passed, I decided to become a musician.

As I am figuring out how to deal with this pandemic, I don't know why, but I think of my grandmother's oldest brother, and I see him as clearly as I use to see him on Sundays when he would stop by to see my grandmother after church.

I don't know what my great uncle's feelings were about me, but since we were a very close family, I assume at a minimum, he didn't dislike me. I know my mother was one of his favorite nieces and maybe the sentiment carried over to me. It is not really important any more. What is important is that when I am back in the county for a visit, when travel and visiting is safe again, I remember what I learned from my strong ancestors.

I don't know why my great uncle is still reaching out to me after seven decades. It is as if he either wants me to tell the world about how my grandmother felt about him, or he wants me to tell the world he had many wonderful things planned when he met his untimely death.

Maybe he wants me to understand and appreciate the opportunity I have to learn and grow doing this pandemic? I don't have anyone to discuss this with now. I have no place to start my inquiries about my old memories. Maybe it is best I can't. Great uncles

and aunts, parents, cousins and old associates, are all gone.

I will deal with this pandemic. I
do wish, however, they had all lived to
be one hundred years, or older.

CHAPTER NINE

MY UNCLE JOE

MY UNCLE JOE

My mother's oldest sister's favorite color was orange. In the mid-1950s to motivate me to pursue the academic life, she took me with her to her college reunion.

From listening to my aunt Cheryl and her college friends talk, I learned while she was in college, aunt Cheryl earned the nickname of Orange, because orange was her favorite color. Her college friends said most everything in her closet was some shade of orange. It was to her college classmates surprise, that after graduation, my aunt Cheryl met and married a man sur named Orange.

My mother's oldest sister's husband was the first uncle I really remember identifying with. Joe Orange was a farmer, a husband and a really great uncle to me. I am sure he was many other fine things, but these were the things that were important to me and they stand out in my memory doing this pandemic.

It was the time when I was about four or five years old that Joe Orange, my mother's oldest sister's husband, began to play a significant role in my life. I am sure he must have been there before I was four or five, but for the life of me, I just can't remember him lifting me out of the crib or feeding me my bottle, although, I am sure he must have done those things for me.

My first real memories of my uncle Joe are of me standing on the truck seat of his 1948 green Chevy pickup truck.

It was a pea green truck with gray cloth seats. This was long before seat belts or safety concerns about children going through the windshield in a sudden crash. During this period, it was a showing of love to have one's children accompany one throughout the work day by standing on the front seat of your car or truck. Even allowing your child to sit on your lap for the child to have the allusion of being the driver was acceptable.

Sitting here this early rainy morning, listening to the ever-rising death tolls from Covit-19, the news about business closures and children not being allowed to return to schools, I flash back to standing on that pickup truck seat until I got tired, stretched out and fell asleep.

Now, I am not so much wishing for those times to return, as much as I desire a senior relative to be in charge and tell me what to do.

The comfort of growing up in a large close-nit farm family takes on more significance than it did before Corvit-19. It is clear to me why my folks thought it necessary to work every day with no regard for the weather, the temperature or the title of the day. Christmas, Thanksgiving, Easter or one's own birthday never presented a cause for not working from sun up to sun down. "Waste not, want not. . ." was the first repetitive phrase I remember learning.

Motivation was not a guiding cause for work, work was something that was just necessary and was never questioned. Having never been able to shake this precept, I understand why I haven't panicked during this pandemic. I am able to plan and I have faith I will successfully make it through, and also grow and prosper.

I learned a lot from riding on the front seat of my mother's oldest sister's husband's pickup truck. Not to ever be in bed when the sun rises seems to be the most important.

With the clock just changing because of day light savings time and the days getting shorter and shorter, I clearly see the logic and necessity of uncle Joe always saying, " . . . come on Claude, let's make hay while the sun shines." This was said about everything uncle Joe and I did together, not just bailing hay.

Simplicity was the watch-word of the day, every day, down on the farm. Today I watch the long lines at the food banks and am somewhat miffed at all of

the fuss. Down home, we grew and pro-
cessed almost everything that we ate, ate
simply and only when it was necessary.
 I find great comfort in measuring two
table spoons of grits into a half cup of
boiling water while waiting for my one
sausage patty to cook and my one egg to
finish frying hard.

Eating in the truck while moving
towards the fields was not the exception,
but the rule. The first thing I figured out
during the early days of the pandemic
was the amount of food I would need for
the next year. Knowing I have it in the
house is quite a comfort.

Hearing uncle Joe's voice saying,
" . . . close that ice box door, turn the
lights off when you leave the room and
don't try to heat up the outside by leaving that door open . . .", not only comes
back to me with clarity, but with understanding.

Minimizing my electric, gas and
water bills, thanks to my uncle Joe, is
something I know how to do. There will
be no need for me to get special payment

plans from the utility companies, I was taught how not to use utilities. Understanding I will not die by sleeping under several quilts in a cold house, and knowing I will not catch a cold when I get up an hour before dressing to turn up the heat is a great comfort to me.

There were times when uncle Joe and I would go overboard in our eating. Some of my fondest memories from my early development are of stopping at the general store at the Cross Roads, a little settlement half way between our little town and his farm, and purchasing a lemon cream pie. Uncle Joe's favorite pie was lemon cream and it became my favorite also.

We would get a couple of cokes or some chocolate milk and head for the farm eating as we drove.

Uncle Joe was known throughout the county for raising and butchering hogs. His reputation extended to the adjoining counties and throughout the eastern part of the state. He also grew tobacco, beans, water melons and other staples, but he was best known for his skill at raising hogs and curing the hams he marketed at the end of the summer season.

When I was 6 or 7 years old uncle Joe and aunt Cheryl were already in their early forties. They didn't have any children and had given up on having any. For uncle Joe, I was the son he never had or expected to have. Turns out he, my aunt Cheryl and the rest of the family were wrong. They did have a son when they were close to fifty.

The timing was perfect, I was headed for high school, was too big to stand up on the seat of the green pickup truck and uncle Joe needed a replacement for me.

I fondly remember my uncle Joe picking me up when we arrived anywhere and proudly displaying me as if I were his own son. But when asked he would say, " . . . no, this is Louise's boy." This representation never made me feel he loved me any less than if I were his own real son.

When uncle Joe got his own son, he had already ushered me into early manhood and he had no trouble doing the same for my cousin..

Using uncle Joe as the example for what I must do to survive and prosper through this pandemic, I picture him as a tall man, because my fondest memories are of him lifting me out of his pea green pickup truck.

This mental picture of a giant of a man has stayed with me over seventy years. However, recalling the realization that hit me just after his death, as I matured into adulthood, I was a couple of inches taller than he was. I also realized I was not the man he was and never would be.

I knew for a while prior to uncle Joe's death my mother's oldest sister's husband would not recover from his illness. During that period, I attempted to let him know, as I had always attempted to do, I appreciated the care and love he had always given me. This effort became hard to nearly impossible. Uncle

Joe's illness affected his mind long before it weakened his body.

I still visited and sat with him as
often as I could, but it became clear he
no longer knew me from anyone else.
This was part of his rights of passage.
He had worked hard, raised two sons and
had earned the right to retreat into a
mentally safe haven.

I can't remember attending my
uncle Joe's funeral. Reflecting doing this
pandemic, I can't remember why I
wouldn't have attended. I don't know
whether I am blocking it out because I
don't want to acknowledge he is actually
dead when I need to consult him and
have him tell me how to make it through
2020, or whether I just didn't go.

I missed a lot of family functions
while I was in the army and out of the
country in Vietnam. Apparently, I have
also blocked out some sad memories, because now that I am the oldest person in
my family line, I just don't want to believe I have no one to turn to for support.

Uncle Joe didn't live to the family standard of 100 years, he only made it into his early seventies.

I don't eat lemon cream pie much anymore, but when I do, I always think of a pea green Chevy pickup truck, my mother's oldest sister's husband, and the lessons I learned standing at his feet.

CHAPTER TEN

MY AUNT PEGGY'S ELOPMENT

MY AUNT PEGGY'S ELOPMENT
By the mid-1950s my mother's sisters had all graduated college, all but one had married and they had scattered to different states. In reality this dispersal for employment purposes extended to southern Mississippi and central Texas.

My maternal family was large and close nit. Five sisters, three brothers and scores of cousins and nondescript hangers-oners. All of the girls went to college and became educators and the boys followed their father into farming.

The nature of secondary school employment meant the girls were not working at their primary occupation three months during school vacation.

They all returned to the farm to help their father harvest the crops.

This was an annual ritual and it held the key, not only to successfully harvesting the crops, but was the most celebrated period of the year for the family, second only to Christmas.

I was the oldest grandchild and the only nephew my mother's sisters and brothers had. This was an honored position for me and one I played with academy award-winning skill. Even though I hated to see the end of the school year because it meant I would have to work on the farm from sun up to sun down six days a week, I was always thrilled to anticipate the return of my aunts and their spouses for the summer.

This regrouping of the clan and the harvesting activities were as predictable as the return of the swallows to Capistrano. It occurred with precision every summer. The actual date and time varied, everyone in the county knew, however, the family would be with their father in the fields doing the harvest.

We never knew what day the 3 car caravan would arrive, but it seemed never to fail that the arrival would be in the hours between mid-night and 4 a.m. It had something to do with the time they left Texas, then driving to Mississippi and then home.

During the years prior to my going to college, they never arrived during the day light hours. This added to the excitement, because when they did arrived. the whole family and some of the neighbors got up and stayed up and talked for the remainder of the night.

It was the unpacking of the cars that was the most fun for me. As good aunts and uncles were suppose to, they always brought plenty of stuff for me, my grandmother and grandfather.

The gifts made it like a mid-year Christmas. Not much went on in our small farming community during the late forties and early fifties, and any positive activities were enjoyed to the max. I got educational toys, books, clothes and enough money to carry me through the summer.

Keep in mind this was before social media and the community telephone was at the local gas station. It was a period when entertainment was considered the devil's enticement and TV stations broad casts only a few hours per day. A book on math was as appreciated and as enjoyed as much as an advanced copy of a first run movie today.

Sitting here alone listening to the ever-increasing numbers of deaths from the virus, the news that President Trump will not acknowledge his loss in the election, the closing of schools and businesses and the dire predictions for the future of the economy, I long for the security I wanted to grow up and get away from when I lived on the family farm.

Of all of those fondly remembered mid-year family reunions, I remember one in particular. It was somewhere around 1957 or 58. I can pin point the time, because that summer my aunt Peggy got her first car, a 1957 Chevrolet Bel Air two door hard top. It had a white top over a pinkish body with an automatic transmission.

The 1957 Chevy remains my favorite car, probably because my mother's knee baby sister, my aunt Peggy, let me drive her new car through the neighborhood. I was not old enough to have a license. She had the confidence I would not wreck it or kill anyone.

Of course, she knew I had been driving the tractor on the farm for several years. She was also aware all farm boys big enough to reach the petals were taught to handle heavy farm equipment. My aunt Peggy put driving license regulations behind my status in the community.

I circled the narrow street through the neighborhood driving slow enough to be seen and so the neighbors could jump out of the way, if I lost control. That summer, I was the little big man. I had not only driven something that didn't have a plow on it, I had driven on a paved public road in a new car.

That year the family had arrived as usual in the middle of the night. They arrived on a Saturday. It was raining heavily. We stayed up talking until the early hours of Sunday morning.

I was always the first to wake up, whether I needed to or not. I got up that morning about 5 a.m. On the farm at this particular time most of the early awakening was, however, absolutely necessary.

It was either the gathering of the eggs, the slopping of the hogs or the cleaning of the house before we headed for the fields that made getting up early mandatory. But on this particular Sunday morning, I had finished my six consecutive days of sun up to sun down labor and didn't have to get up a minute before 6:30 a.m. But, as still is my habit, even in this pandemic, on this particular Sunday, I was up and dressed at 5 a.m.

It was raining like it does in the middle of the monsoon season in Southeast Asia. I loved rainy days back then,

especially on days other than Sundays.
If the rain was accompanied by lighten-
ing, we wouldn't go into the fields.
However, if it was just rain, even very
hard rain, the feeding of the pigs and the
harvesting of the crops still had to go on.

The early morning hours were
perfect. I would read, think and plan
how I would one day graduate high
school and leave the county for good, for
better or worst, but definitely forever.

On this particular morning I
awoke to the sounds of rain falling on
our tin roof. This is one of the sounds I
miss the most from the farm.' During
this pandemic hearing rain falling on a
tin roof would help me remain calm and
plan my way through the unknown dan-
gers. If my aunts and uncles were here,
they could just tell me what to do.

I am sure it rained again before I
left home, but even when I turn off the
news, I can't remember enjoying the
sounds of rain on a tin roof ever again.

When I awoke, I made my way
down stairs, through the dining room

and into the kitchen. With my glass of
cold water in hand, I headed back to the
TV room and sat down. I would have
turned on the TV, but at that time in the
morning there was no station broadcast-
ing.

After a few minutes of fingering
my book, I looked at the top of the TV
set, and saw an envelope addressed to
the family.

Even though we never locked the
doors, or had a house key, no one would
have just walked into the house during
the night and left an envelope. I knew it
had to be put there by someone inside.
Opening the envelope, I read the hand
written note signed by my aunt Peggy.

The note began by apologizing
for not telling the family in person what
she was about to say. Aunt Peggy wrote
she had fallen in love and had gotten
married two weeks earlier. She said she
had left in the middle of the night to
drive back to Mississippi to be with her
new husband.

My aunt Peggy was the last of

my mother's siblings to get married and for some reason felt the family would not approve of her choice. She didn't say this in the note, but I knew my aunt Peggy and I understood this was what she was thinking. This was particularly strange, because her father would never have addressed her choice, either positive or negative. My grandfather always minded his own business and when one of his adult children made a decision, he just supported them. This was true, whether he approved or not. This was the family way.

Whenever I would bring a lady home and tell my family I liked her, they would just say, " . . . Junior, that's your bear, we don't have to sleep with her."

Well, after reading the note I ran through the house and woke everybody up. "Aunt Peggy has run away". I screamed. I passed the note to my mother and she passed it to the rest of the family. We all just laughed, then wished her well.

It was the consensus it had been

so cray for her to elope. She was in her
early thirties and knew everyone would
have welcomed and approved of her
choice, no matter how bad the choice
may have been.

Aunt Peggy's younger sister
knew the new husband. She thought he
was a nice enough fellow, a fairly well-
off peach farmer known for raising cattle
and making molasses from his sugar
cane.

The only thing the family could-
n't figure out was why my aunt Peggy
figured the family would be upset. The
man she had married was much older
than she was. No one actually cared
though, they just wanted her to have a
safe trip back to Mississippi and enjoy
her new life.

It was a long hot hard summer on
the farm that year. The work was particularly difficult, because my aunt Peggy
wasn't there. This is better understood,
when I tell you my Aunt Peggy was not
only a hard and willing worker in the
fields, but she could do the work of any

two men and a small boy.

That summer passed, nothing else happened worth remembering during this pandemic. The family remained intact and over the years, we all went to visit the big unpainted farm house my aunt Peggy and her husband lived in.

As was the family custom when we visited, we picked peaches from his trees, hauled tin cans of molasses from his processing house and acted as if he was the best thing that could have happened to my aunt.

Old uncle Samuel (. . . and as it turned out, he was much older that aunt Peggy) never did visit our family farm, but his younger brother and his wife visited often.

I don't remember seeing uncle Samuel more than once or twice. I graduated high school, went to college and got drafted into the Army.

It appears that my aunt was correct when she assumed she had made a move the family wouldn't have approved when she married uncle Samuel. I don't know how long the marriage lasted, but it wasn't too long before they went their separate ways. I think they grew tired of each other within four or five years, divorced, but remained friends until uncle Samuel died in the mid-1960s. I often wondered what happened to all of those peach trees and that big unpainted farm house.

Aunt Peggy lived about twenty-five years after the divorce. She and I never talked about the morning I awoke and found her note. I always meant to sit down and talk to her about it, but I never did. It was the family way, we always minded our own business.

My aunt Peggy and I were very close. She would do anything she could for me and she lived long enough for me to repay many of her kindnesses.

She retired and moved back to the family farm. She grew relatively old, contracted cancer, fought it for a while and lost the battle.

Whenever I sat with her, we talked about the old days on the farm, about how she had taught me to read at a very early age, and how the time had made us both older and wiser. But we never talked about either her failed marriage or mine. This was the family way.

I learned after my aunt Peggy's death she appreciated the things I had tried to do for her in appreciation for the thing. she had done for me.

After her funeral, the administrator of her estate informed me I was named her sole beneficiary. It surprised the hell out of me, I never figured my aunt Peggy would die before she reached the age of 100. She was just seventy when she elected to go to her eternal reward. I am glad she shared all of those years with me.

As I sit here wondering when the world will open up, I sense my aunt Peggy sitting here with me, telling me I am going to be OK, and I just need to get up early each morning, plan, work hard and keep the family ways.

CHAPTER ELEVEN

MY SECOND AUNT GEORGIA

MY SECOND AUNT GEORGIA

My maternal grandmother had a sister named Georgia. The name is only important when it is put into the context of my having two great aunts named Georgia.

My maternal grandfather also had a sister named Georgia. Strange for the family, neither aunt Georgia had a distinguishing nick name. This did not present a problem in identifying them though. My grandfather almost never spoke of his wife's, my grandmother's sister, and for reasons still unknown to me, my grandmother never spoke of or visited her husband's sister Georgia.

So, we always immediately knew the aunt Georgia referenced by the person mentioning the name.

My maternal grandmother's sister Georgia's house was the destination of many of our family's Sunday evening outings, so I got to visit this great aunt Georgia quite often. I never remember, however, developing much of a relationship with her.

I look back during this pandemic and see there wasn't much reason for me to have developed a relationship with her. I was a very young child in a time and place where children were to be seen and not heard. I was also two generations removed.

I vividly remember the great aunt Georgia that was my maternal grandmother's sister looked a lot like my grandmother, but she was not as pretty.

As was the custom in the county, my grandmother's sister Georgia dipped snuff. This was long before tobacco products were considered not only harmful to one's health, but also disgusting when used as a powder and repeatedly spit out without regard to where you or anyone with you was standing.

Dipping snuff tended to be a ra-

ther unobjectionable habit in our little tobacco growing community. I never liked
the dipping habit much when I was a
child, because the people who used it
had to spit out a gross looking brown
colored substance at regular intervals.
Even while riding in an automobile, stuff
users carried a tin cup to spit in and this
literally turned my stomach.

For those who are unacquainted
with the habit of dipping snuff, it was a
finely ground tobacco powder that was
placed in the lower lip. The user always
had a protruding pouch on one side of
their face and constantly used their index
finger to move it around. A lot of people
used it in the old days either out of not
knowing of the danger of lip cancer or
out of allegiance to their main financial
source of support. Tobacco was king
and it was the dominant cash crop for
county farmers.

Sitting here as an adult trying to
figure out how to make it through this
pandemic, I realize I made a distinction
between my relatives who used tobacco

in one form or another and those who
did not. However, I also realize, I
tended not to mind or notice the disgusting habit in my relatives who I liked a
lot, because they paid special attention to
me. It is clear I was doing this in an in-
appropriate judgmental way. I considered the use of tobacco products a sign
of weakness.

Looking at the use of illegal
drugs and excess use of alcohol today, I
am beginning to think the use of tobacco
products by my seniors was just a minor
coping mechanism. With the strict racism and unapologetic denial of jobs they
had to live with, I see the strength it took
to restrict one's bad habits to just tobacco
use.

Well, my grandmother's sister
Georgia used tobacco in the form of
snuff every waking moment of every
single day. The only time I recall seeing
her without the customary pouched
lower lip filled with snuff was in church.
Even in tobacco country in the late

1940s and early 50s using tobacco anywhere near a church, especially a Southern Baptist Church, was considered just not right.

I think I remember my grandfather's sister Georgia using snuff also, but I never got to know her enough to like or dislike her on that basis.

Having plenty of time to reflect between the Covid-19 mortality reports, I realize I really didn't have enough time with my grandmother's sister Georgia to know whether I liked her or not. This realization will certainly help me in going forward and not drawing uninformed opinions of people either positive or negative.

On the Sunday evenings I spent with my maternal grandmother visiting her sister Georgia, it is clear, I just sat quietly on the corner of her living room sofa.

It was the custom doing Sunday visits to anyone's house to sit in the living room, it was always the best room in the house, and only used to entertain guests. It is without question, one of the major goals in the county was to grow to senior status, have your own living room set, cover it with plastic and always keep it looking as new as if it was just off loaded from the Sears and Roebuck delivery truck. My maternal grandmother's sister Georgia was no exception to this rule. In addition to her perfectly kept living room, she had no children and a husband.

Looking back it seems to me my great aunt Georgia tried to like me on those occasions when I visited her with her sister. On those Sunday evenings, there was very little reason for her to put much effort into me. I was only her sister's second daughter's child. Although I was the apple of my grandmother's eye, I was probably just a leaf on the family tree for my maternal great aunt Georgia and she knew I would in time just fall off the tree and blow away.

Looking back, I hope she didn't observe the way I squinted every time she would pick up her Maxwell House coffee can to expel her snuff. If she did, maybe that is why I never was her favorite. She also may not have wanted little kids in her house, since she didn't have any.

My maternal great aunt Georgia never worked outside of the house and all of her efforts went into maintaining the museum-like appearance of her home. Other peoples' children were probably just a temporary annoyance for her. I will never know. All of my senior relatives who lived in the county at the time are either dead or have entered the realm of the alive, but memory-less.

Even if I can't find out the answers to my many questions about my family history, it really doesn't matter now. Since everyone is with the angels and I am trying to survive Covid-19 and not join them just yet, I should turn my thoughts to figuring out what I need to do to fit into this New World Order.

Anyway, I guess my grandmother's sister Georgia was never my fa-

vorite since she had such tough competi-
tion for my juvenile affections. Not that
it was a contest either great aunt Georgia
, or even I, knew about. It just turned
out some of my other great aunts, aunts,
great uncles and uncles had more time
and energy to dedicate to me.

It has taken me over seventy
years to realize my maternal grandmother's sister Georgia was doing the
best she could for me and everyone else.
I realize there are younger family members than I am now and they hold the
same relationship to me as I held to my
maternal grandmother's sister Georgia.
They will look at and judged me the
same way I may have unfairly judge my
grandmother's sister Georgia. I should
just be more careful about how I am re-
lating to these junior family members.

I compared my maternal great
aunt Georgia with the wife of my maternal great uncle Fred's wife Edna. This
was not a fair or reasoable thing for me
to do. I was comparing a woman who
had no children and wanted none, to a

woman who had no children and wanted some, and made me her own.

There was one particular Sunday in the early 1950s when my grandmother's sister Georgia asked if I liked chocolate cake. I responded yes, and she promised to make me one. I saw her the last time at Christmas in 1972, she had not made me that cake, even though I said yes, and she promised it to me.

For over sixty years I consciously have held not getting that cake, a cake I didn't solicit, against my maternal great aunt Georgia.

Whenever I thought about her, I pictured the missing, never delivered, chocolate cake. I better learn to forgive great aunt Georgia before I pass on myself. I clearly see she had many more important things on her mind than making me that cake.

Just because my great aunt Edna always delivered her cakes when promised, I was not the apple of everyone else's eye.

My maternal great aunt Georgia,

who never made me that chocolate cake, died at slightly less than one hundred years of age. I doubt she remembered me or the cake. I am almost over not getting that cake now, and stepping very close to eighty myself, I better get over it soon.

Even though I am trying with every breath to reach the family 100 year standard as most of my relatives did, I will have to work harder to make it with this pandemic. This crona virus is certainly not helping my chances.

Even if I fall short of the family standard and make it only 15 or 20 or so more years, I will probably be happier, if I finally forgive my maternal great aunt Georgia for not making that chocolate cake.

Having thought of this for over seventy years, moving passed it with less non-relevant emotional baggage will make the rest of my trip through this plane, however long it may be, just a little easier.

EPILOGUE

In the deep South in the late 1940s white restaurant owners hadn't as yet figured out that Negroes, as blacks were officially classified then, were one-half of the population and if allowed to eat in segregated cafes profits would double.

In rural farming communities with only agricultural employment, the physical labor required a hardy healthy breakfast and a big mid-day meal.

A convenient and commercially available food source for the mostly black labor force would have been, not only an economic boom to white businesses, but nourishment-deficient meals would have created the health crisis a half century earlier for the black community that all communities suffers from today.

As you can see, I am looking for the good that is always contained in the bad.

Fortunately, good old Jim Crow, or racial bias, kept local prejudiced food service proprietors from gaining financial success and delayed medically deprived Negro communities the later inflicted obesity, diabetes, high blood pressure and related negative health conditions minority and majority communities suffer from today.

As I listen to the Covid-19 restrictions placed on restaurants, bars and social gatherings of all types, I am emotionally unaffected.

Having come-up in the segregated South during a period when restaurants, major entertainment and sports facilities were closed to me because of the color of my skin, I have continued to follow the old ways taught to me by the giants who prepared me to live in this jungle, survive and prosper, because of, not in-spite of, institutionalized racism.

I typically cook and eat all of my meals at home, prepare a traveling-lunch when I am transiting by plane or car, and only participate in commercial entertainment functions when necessary to ac-

commodate the likes of a very, very special lady.

Listening to crying-failing-busi-
ness owners during this pandemic, I am
receptive and understanding of their loss.
However, my personal recent negative
experiences with high-end restaurants
and commercial establishments while
dressed in conservative tailor-made
suits, initialed silk shirts and displaying
university rings, causes me to question
their sincerity when they now use the
word WE.

I have often, and recently, been
asked, if I was sure I had reservations or
whether I was absolutely certain I was in
the right establishment. Now, I am assured that WE are in this pandemic TO-
GETHER.

I have been taught to seek out the
positives in negative situations and capi-
talize on them. We are all certainly in a
negative situation with this pandemic.
Unfortunately, I can pin point the exact
time that the THOSE PEOPLE disappeared and became a WE.

It is my hope that WE will all look back and consider what and who WE have done wrong in the past, who WE have judged inappropriately and why, and learn.

I have not come through the last seven decades with any hate for those who have discriminated willfully against ME because of the color of my skin.

I have encouraged prejudiced people to just look a little closer at me and they will find plenty of other reasons to dislike me, and be justified in doing so.

To the employers, business owners, my associates and anyone else who did not consider me in the same boat THEY were in prior to the pandemic, I wish THEM the best. However, I will be observing THEIR actions after the pandemic, and if THEY observe that I withhold my business from THEM, I hope THEY remember when THEY said WE-WERE-ALL-IN-THE-SAME-BOAT-TOGETHER.

Understanding the reality of this

nation and the world coming to grips with a disease that is not racially exclusive and takes one and all, I can't forget after the return to normal black troops are systematically relegated to second class citizenship, even though allowed to keep and display earned Medals of Honor.

After periods of universal danger are over, economically successful black business persons are again immediately denied the right to purchase a house in a restricted neighborhood and are carefully and intentionally fitted under the glass sealing.

I am neither bitter or envious of the achievements of those who now find their businesses in need of government stimulus. I fully support those who have managed to achieve great wealth by providing entertainment to those of us who elect to pay several hundred dollars to attend an entertainment event, while leaving our children in the care of a minimum wage baby sitter.

It is more than acceptable to me

that the greatest financial reward is given to those of us who reach adulthood and excel at playing children's games. The dedication it takes to develop skills in sports and entertainment must be rewarded.

My concern and sympathies, however, don't go to the touring performers, or the recently drafted foot ball and basket ball players who are loosing their salaries because factory workers, government clerks, truck drivers and school teachers can no longer afford tickets.

I am more than saddened when I drive through the center of a city and see block after block of decorative electric signs being removed from sports and entertainment complexes.

I am not unaware of the loss of the jobs of custodians who work part time cleaning up after major events. I have friends and associates who work a second job at sporting complexes to afford rent and mortgage payments.

When those who have supported

Broadway plays, championship play-
offs, title fights and racing car competi-
tions no longer have the resources to
participate in well-deserved positive re-
laxing experiences, it is truly a great
loss.

Sitting here contemplating how
to replace my own reduction of financial
under-pending caused by the closure of
universities, businesses that no longer
need consulting services or don't exist at
all, I share the pain.

The necessity of non-necessary
social activities has never been clearer to
me. When there is a restriction on
travel, there are fewer people for the po-
lice to arrest for drunk driving, this reduces the number of alcoholics who re-
quire counseling, leaves unused parking
lots near court houses and reduces the
number of parking attendants needed to
process cars in an out, causes my cousin
to be laid off from her job at the auto re-
pair shop and increases the probability
she will come to me and explain why she
has not repaid the last loan and needs

help again.

Rechecking the last seven decades to analyzing the people and conditions that have shaped my ability to face this Covid-19 storm, I approach each minute, each hour and each half-day with the absolute position that I must survive and prosper.

I have faced the fact there will never be a return to NORMAL. What I had come to accept and claim as my well deserve status in the employment, social, family and economic structure of society is gone, never to return in the same form.

As for employment, I, and the rest of the world, must accept that the old regular recognized 9 to 5 is gone. The 7:30 a.m. trolley rolls no more. The trolley engineer caught Covid-19, went to the hospital and died. Her replacement wore a mask, but got sick anyway. Then the next replacement was fired because of the lack of ridership.

The receptionist with the lovely smile who staffed the front desk and made sure everyone had a cup of coffee is no longer needed. There isn't 6 feet from the door to his desk. The new TV monitor is staffed by a non-gender voice in another city. We don't know which city, it changes from day to day.

Clients can't meet us at the office any more. The table in the conference room is only five feet four inches long and there is no ventilation system that meets CDC standards.

Even though the office is on the second floor, clients, most of whom are elderly and disabled, can't negotiate the steps. The elevator is only safe for one person because of its small size. In a 9 story building with thousands of occupants, even getting up and arriving early, we can't predicted when the down trip can be safely made.

A recognition of the demise and non-resurrection of the old-accepted-normal will take major adjustments for us, mentally, physically and financially. To recognize, accept and then take this new knowledge and develop the skills and habits to re-establish ourselves in the

ever-changing social networks in which
constant newness will be the New Normal is possible, but it will not be easy.

Stability, predictability and non-
perceivable change have been the guide-
lines by which we, and the rest of the
world, have based our lives.

We have all known whose bottom to kiss, whose boots to lick and
what person or organizations we have
had to pay homage to keep our jobs,
maintain our social standing in formal
and informal social circles, and guaran-
tee our entry into the financial networks
that allowed the mortgage/rent to be
paid, groceries to be secured, clothes to
be selected, cleaned and replaced at regular intervals, attend entertainment
events, enjoy the aftergame dinner and
drinks that until March of 2020 were absolutely necessary for a normal life.

Now we have the New Normal.
We wake up each day and turn on the
morning news to determine if overnight
we ourselves died in the waiting room of
the local hospital, because there was no

available bed. The biblical phrase, " . . . no room at the Inn. . ." now takes on a meaning even the nonreligious under-stand.

Weather WE are some color that is not white or whether WE are as white as the snow that has promised to bring even more Covid-19 deaths this winter, each and every one of US now knows the feeling of being rejected at the "Inn" or "hospital", because there is a disease that has no respect for color or financial status.

It is still to be seen whether available rooms at the hospital will again be systematically and system wide de-nied to those of color when things return to a NORMAL.

For me it has been a consistent observation that with great universal danger WE all become EQUAL.

The house that the realtor did not want to show or sell me last year, I am now welcomed to purchase without a court suit and with no money down. The neighbor who drove by without waiving over the years WE have shared the same block, now toots his horn as he passes by. My cousin that ignored me for the last five years now asks about the things I was interested in providing him then, but am saving for myself now.

Here WE are, the old-normal-monkey who was on our backs has turned into a giant gorilla with an unlimited thirst for anything that sustains our lives.

WE find OUR friendship previously rejected is now sought after. When I get texts, emails and phone messages from those who made it clear when THEY were on the rise and didn't have time to be concerned with my welfare, but are checking to see how I am doing in this pandemic, I sense that THEY have the sudden realization that there is a new found understanding that WE really are in this boat together and that I may be able to take the oars and row, when THEY can't.

This New Normal definitely will demand an enhanced acceptance, not only among restaurant and business owners, barbers, cosmetologists, air plane pilots, doctors, artists and entertainers, that their former vision of where THEY stood in relationship to others in society may not have been as superior as THEY thought.

Family members who had rejected us, friends who had been more successful than us and had eliminated us from their circle of acceptable associates now are considering whether the size of THEIR social bubble just might need to be increased.

Having experienced the down turns of a failed marriage, the life changing events caused by required-family absence because of war, unanticipated employment losses, as well as, just bad luck, I am not unacquainted with the flight of employers, family, friends and associates to the hills, when I am in the valley of despair.

Because my ancestors have guided me during their lifetimes, and now allow me to draw from the secrets they taught me, I know I am prepared to weather this Covid-19 storm.

Not only am I confident I can face the winds coming from normal and yet underdetermined directions and bend when necessary without breaking, I also know I have sat at the feet of my ancestors who have made it under even more difficult circumstances, and they passed their secrets to me.

Looking back to how my ancestors taught me to treat food as a necessity and to respect it by consuming no more than is necessary to maintain my health, I have secured enough household items to maintain without going to the grocery store for an indefinite period.

Analyzing my financial status, I have made changes that will enable me to survive the economic down turn whether it last months or years.

My ancestors have passed to me the secrets of those who have broken the chains of slavery, faced the uneven laws of racial discrimination, and overcome the injustices of the denial of human rights, because the majority sought equality by denying equality to others.

I, at this time of only partial social injustice, have no excuse to not survive, prosper and shape the New World Order to my benefit.

Through times significantly worst than what we are experiencing yet you don't know no with Covid-19, most of my ancestors lived to be 100 years old or older.

THIS IS THE REASON I WILL BEAT THIS PANDEMIC!